DATE DUE

Annika SORENSTAM

By Bob Woods

The **Child's World**

www.childsworld.com

Published in the United States of America by The Child's World®
P.O. Box 326 • Chanhassen, MN 55317-0326
800-599-READ • www.childsworld.com

ACKNOWLEDGMENTS

The Child's World®: Mary Berendes, Publishing Director

Produced by Shoreline Publishing Group LLC
President / Editorial Director: James Buckley, Jr.
Designer: Tom Carling, carlingdesign.com
Assistant Editors: Jim Gigliotti, Ellen Labrecque

Photo Credits
Cover: Corbis.
Interior: AP/Wide World: 8, 12, 22, 27, 28; Corbis: 5, 14, 15, 17, 24, 26;
Getty Images: 1, 3, 7, 10, 18, 21, 25.

LIBRARY OF CONGRESS
CATALOGING-IN-PUBLICATION DATA

Woods, Bob.
  Annika Sorenstam / by Bob Woods.
     p. cm. — (The world's greatest athletes)
  Includes bibliographical references and index.
  ISBN-13: 978-1-59296-788-9 (library bound : alk. paper)
  ISBN-10: 1-59296-788-4 (library bound : alk. paper)
  1. Sorenstam, Annika, 1970——Juvenile literature. 2. Women
golfers—Sweden—Biography—Juvenile literature. 3. Golfers—
Sweden—Biography—Juvenile literature. I. Title. II. Series.

  GV964.S63W66 2007
  796.352092—dc22
  [B]

                                        2006031554

CONTENTS

The Greatest Female Golfer Ever

SAYING THAT ANYONE OR ANYTHING IS "THE greatest ever" can be a tough thing to prove. Whether you're talking about athletes, movie stars, cars, or candy bars, everyone has an opinion about who or what is greater than the other. Sometimes it's simply a matter of taste. Just because you love chocolate ice cream more than any other flavor doesn't make it the greatest ever—especially for your best friend, who loves vanilla better.

It's difficult to argue, however, against Annika Sorenstam (pronounced "AHN-ih-kuh SOR-in-stahm") being called the greatest female golfer ever. Just consider what the sensation from Sweden had accomplished by the age of 35 entering the 2007 season:

• She won 69 tournaments, good for third place on the all-time LPGA (Ladies **Professional** Golf Association) career victories list.

• She won 10 "major" tournaments—the four most prestigious events held annually on the LPGA Tour.

• She earned eight LPGA Player of the Year awards, the most ever.

• She won six career Vare Trophies (awarded for the lowest scoring average for the season).

Here's a familiar sight: Annika holding up a championship trophy.

Even Annika herself can hardly believe how great a golfer she really is. "I feel like I'm just a little girl from Sweden who came over here to follow my dreams and hope to win a few golf tournaments. When I look at my bio in the LPGA book, I get overwhelmed."

Indeed, the story of Annika Sorenstam is truly overwhelming.

CHAPTER 1

Trading Racquets for Clubs

ANNIKA IS THE OLDER OF TWO DAUGHTERS RAISED by Tom and Gunilla Sorenstam. Born October 9, 1970, near Stockholm, the capital of (and the largest city in) Sweden, Annika was an active, athletic youngster. She and her younger sister, Charlotta, loved to ski, as do many kids in snowy **Scandinavian** countries. Annika also became an excellent tennis player, even thinking about turning professional someday.

That was before she discovered the game of golf when she was 12. Annika got her start at the Bro-Balsta Golf Club, a course near her home. At 15, she began taking lessons from Henri Reis, a famous instructor then with the Swedish Golf Federation. Soon after, Annika put her racquets—and tennis ambitions—away and turned all her attention to golf.

"The thing that made Annika different was that she loved to practice, even more than play," Reis, who is still one of her coaches, told *Golf Digest* magazine. "In a short time, she proved she wanted to succeed more than the other players her age. Annika had this great desire to improve. You can still see that today. She has taken women's golf to a new level, and she continues to work to get better."

Annika's coach, Henri Reis (left), helped her make the transition from tennis standout to full-time golfer.

Annika's skills took one more giant leap forward when she became a member of the Swedish National Team and added Pia Nilsson, another Swedish golf expert, to her team of teachers. Nilsson paved Annika's way to a golf **scholarship** at Arizona State University, where Nilsson had played for four years.

Nilsson's prize pupil quickly swung to the head of the class at ASU. As a 19-year-old freshman, Annika led her team to the 1991 NCAA (National Collegiate Athletic Association) women's national championship and shared the College Player of the Year award. Annika's game improved so rapidly that she left ASU after her sophomore year to pursue her dream of becoming a professional golfer.

Before breaking into the LPGA full time, Annika spent 1993 playing on the Ladies European Tour. She competed in 10 tournaments, came in second in four of them, and was named the

Younger sister Charlotta (left) is a successful LPGA player, too.

Young Annika Sorenstam

► Annika was born to golf. "My mother played golf while she was pregnant with me," she writes in her book *Golf Annika's Way*. "I know I picked up the rhythm of her swing before I was born."

► The Sorenstams were "sports crazy and super competitive," Annika remembers of growing up in Sweden with her parents and younger sister, Charlotta. In addition to golf, the family enjoyed tennis, snow skiing, volleyball, and badminton.

► Annika was a terrific tennis player as a kid. She attended tennis camp every summer from age 5 to 11. At 10, she was one of Stockholm's top 10 players in her age group. Her idol was fellow Swede Bjorn Borg, whose outstanding career included five straight men's titles at Wimbledon (1976–1980).

► As a member of the Swedish National Golf Team from 1987 to 1992, Annika played tournaments in England, Portugal, Spain, and Italy. She first gained international attention at 17, when she led the team to the Junior European Championship.

tour's Rookie of the Year. The 22-year-old sensation also debuted on the LPGA Tour in '93, finishing in the top 10 in two of the three events she entered. While Annika still counts tennis among her hobbies—along with cooking and listening to music—she no doubt had found her true love on the golf course.

CHAPTER 2

Bursting Onto the LPGA Scene

ANNIKA'S SUCCESS IN EUROPEAN TOURNAMENTS convinced her that she was more than ready to perform on the biggest, most competitive stage in international women's golf: the LPGA Tour. Even so, she did not make an **auspicious** debut as a full-time member of the tour, failing to "make the cut" at a tournament in Florida in February 1994. (After two days, most pro tournaments "cut" the full field to those players who still have a reasonable chance to win. Usually it's 60 or 70 players.)

The golf world finally got a good look at the Swedish newcomer during the Women's British Open in August. Maybe she felt comfortable being back in England, where she and her family had lived for three years, because she certainly played like she

There were high fives all around as Annika celebrated her first career victory at the 1995 U.S. Women's Open.

belonged there. Annika stayed close to the leaders all weekend before fellow Swede Liselotte Neumann pulled away for the win with a four-round total score of 280. Annika's 283 was good for a tie for second place with Dottie Mochrie.

When the season ended in December, Annika had competed in 18 tournaments, made the cut in 14, and finished in the top 10 three times. Not only did she earn $127,451, but also Rookie of the Year honors!

At the 1995 U.S. Women's Open—the oldest and toughest of the tour's majors—Annika celebrated the first of her many LPGA victories. She arrived at the **renowned** Broadmoor Golf Club's East Course, in Colorado Springs, Colorado, having already won two European Tour events and earning seven LPGA top-10 finishes.

Annika led the U.S. Open field on Friday, stumbled on Saturday, and stood five strokes behind leader Meg Mallon at the first tee on Sunday. Then Meg fell apart on the front nine (the first nine holes on an 18-hole course), with a bogey on the third hole and a triple-bogey on the **par**-3 fourth. (Each hole is assigned a par, meaning the number of shots a player figures to make before her ball goes in the hole. If it takes her one shot more than par, that's scored a bogey, two shots more is double-bogey, and so on.) Meanwhile, Annika played well and, despite bogeys on 15 and 16, led Meg by one shot after 18. Meg missed a birdie (one shot under par) putt on 18 that would have given the two golfers a tie score.

"It took me a few seconds to realize what had happened," Annika wrote in her 2004 book, *Golf Annika's Way*, recalling her immediate reaction. "At

In 1995, Annika became the first European player ever to be named the LPGA's Player of the Year.

In Her Own Words

On overcoming pressure with confidence:

▶ *"I still get butterflies on the first tee. I still get sweaty hands, and my heart pumps a lot going down the 18th. But I know what winning is all about now, and that's a feeling that I like."*

On the bright red golf shoes a usually modest Annika wore during the 2002 Kraft Nabisco Tournament, which she won for the second year in a row:

▶ *"I really don't know why I put them on. I was thinking about changing after the turn [halfway through her round] because I became quite distracted."*

On the benefits of staying in great physical shape:

▶ *"I've worked hard to craft a swing that's simple and repeatable, but my workouts have also contributed to my success. My strength gave me the endurance to win eight LPGA titles in 2001, 11 in 2002, and six more in 2003. My strength gave me the power to drive the ball more than 270 yards and the confidence to compete against the world's best male players at the 2003 Colonial."*

On her reputation for being too serious and methodical on the golf course:

▶ *"A lot of people think I am cold and have no feelings. But I do. I just try very hard to focus and not let my emotions take over on the golf course."*

The best female golfer in the world shares a laugh with the best male golfer in the world, Tiger Woods, before a round in 2005.

age 24, in just my second year on tour, I had won my first LPGA tournament—and it was the U.S. Open!"

Annika notched two more wins that magical season. When it was over, she had become the first European named LPGA Player of the Year, and the first international player to win the Vare Trophy. And the Annika Era was just beginning.

CHAPTER 3

A Major Question for Annika

ALONG WITH ANNIKA'S EARLY SUCCESS CAME big-time pressure. She experienced plenty of both over the next five years. From 1996 to 2000, Annika won 20 tournaments, set numerous LPGA records, piled up millions of dollars in earnings, and reaped the respect and admiration of her fellow golfers on the tour. Off the golf course, Annika met a very special admirer, David Esch, whom she married in 1997 (though they divorced in 2005).

As much as she enjoyed her growing fame and fortune, Annika paid a heavy price. She lived with constant **scrutiny** from the media, and with high expectations to keep playing at the superstar level. Shy and modest by nature, at times Annika grew uncomfortable with all the attention and lack

The majors bring out fans young and old to watch Annika play.
Here, she tees off in the McDonald's LPGA Championship.

of privacy. Plus, the competition kept rising, as a
new generation of young, talented female golfers
emerged.

A highpoint for Annika occurred at the 1996 U.S.
Open, contested at the Pine Needles Lodge and Golf
Club in Southern Pines, North Carolina. She had tied

for second at the year's first major tournament, the Nabisco Dinah Shore, and tied for 14th at the second, the LPGA Championship. Despite those mixed results, by early June she felt ready to defend her '95 Open title.

Annika had little trouble en route to her second U.S. Open win in 1996.

She proved to be more than ready. On almost every drive off the tee, Annika's ball landed in the short grass of the fairways and avoided the rough, the higher-grass areas on either side. Her putting on the greens was nearly **flawless**, too. Leading by three strokes on Sunday's final round, "I entered that magical zone where every shot goes where you want it to go," she recalled in *Golf Annika's Way*. She birdied the eighth hole for a six-shot lead, nailed a 35-foot putt on the 10th, and then made LPGA history on the final hole.

Annika's six-foot par putt on the 18th green gave her an eight-under-par score of 272. It was the lowest-ever total score in the U.S. Women's Open.

"To win once is wonderful, to win it twice is more than wonderful," an overjoyed Annika told reporters afterward. "I won last year because Meg [Mallon] faltered. This year I won because I played well, and that means a lot more."

However odd it might seem, winning those back-to-back majors led to some of Annika's low points. She admits that achieving so much in such a short time took away part of her incentive to keep improving. She lost focus.

Annika won more LPGA tournaments (18) than anyone else during the 1990s. But she stopped winning the big ones. Whether it's fair or not, golfers are judged on how well they do in the major tournaments. For LPGA players, those are the Kraft Nabisco Championship, the LPGA Championship, the U.S. Women's Open, and the Women's British Open. After her historic U.S. Open win in 1996, Annika suffered through a five-year **drought** before winning another major. And after each loss, no matter how well she played, the questions **lingered**: What's wrong with Annika? She eventually came up with an answer, loud and clear.

"Golf can be frustrating at times," she admits. "But improvement comes only with time and hard work. Once you accept that there are no quick fixes, you'll get more out of the game. You'll get the satisfaction that comes from working hard at something rewarding."

CHAPTER 4

The Queen of Swing

BEGINNING IN 2001, A NEW AND IMPROVED Annika showed up and took control of the LPGA Tour. She regained her mental focus and the drive to play her absolute best every time out. During the offseason, she had practiced extra hard to improve her putting. Every day, she worked with her good friend and Senior PGA (Professional Golfers Association) star Dave Stockton, an expert putter.

The fruits of her hard labor were immediate and dramatic. She burst out of the gate with two solid second-place finishes, then ripped off four straight wins (tying the LPGA record for consecutive wins). During the second tournament, the Standard Register Ping, she recorded a 13-under-par 59—the lowest score ever for a professional female golfer.

No other woman golfer in the world can match Annika's intensity and focus. Here, she lines up a putt.

A week later, Annika snapped her streak without a major win, topping the field at the Nabisco Championship by three strokes. For a jaw-dropping **encore**, at the Office Depot tournament, she roared back from 10 shots down on the final day to beat South Korean Mi Hyun Kim in a playoff. That tied the LPGA record for the biggest comeback victory ever.

The Nabisco Championship winner traditionally takes a dip in the pond by the 18th green. Annika has done it three times!

Even though Annika completed that remarkable 2001 season with eight wins and a half-dozen second-place finishes, she wasn't satisfied. During the offseason, she launched a new fitness program and worked her body into incredible shape. Several days a week she endured a series of exercises—including up to 1,000 crunches, a type of sit-up—weightlifting, and other **rigorous** activities.

Annika's extra muscle and strength paid off in 2002. She added nearly 15 yards to her drives, which helped power her to an LPGA-record-tying 11 victories in 23 tournaments. One of the sweetest was a repeat win at the Kraft Nabisco Championship for her fourth major title.

Feeling confident, happy, relaxed, and pretty much unbeatable, in 2003 Annika took on what she's called "the biggest challenge of my life": playing against men in a PGA tournament. No woman had done so since Babe Didrikson Zaharias in 1945 (before becoming a champion golfer, Babe was a track and field gold medalist at the 1932 Olympic Games), and several PGA players criticized Annika's bold decision, saying she couldn't compete with men.

So all eyes were on the only player with a

Men's pro Jesper Parnevik, a fellow Swede, joined Annika for a practice round before the 2003 Bank of America Colonial.

ponytail teeing off at the Bank of America Colonial tournament Fort Worth, Texas, in May. The onlookers included Phil Mickelson, Sergio Garcia, Nick Price, and 107 other male golfers—11 of whom she ended up beating as the crowds cheered her every shot. However, after playing two solid rounds of 71 and 74

The Lowdown on "59"

The Sorenstams had a thing about the Standard Register Ping event as the new millennium unfolded. In 2000, Charlotta, the younger of the two sisters on the tour, claimed her very first LPGA win at that annual tournament. A year later, the siblings were paired on the second day. That's when Annika became the first woman in LPGA history to shoot a round under 60. For good measure, she won the event by breaking the LPGA's 72-hole scoring record, finishing 27 under par for a total score of 261.

Annika began her record-breaking round at the 534-yard 10th hole at Moon Valley Country Club in Phoenix, Arizona, with a birdie. Then came another, and another, and another . . . until she'd birdied eight in a row. After a par, Annika ripped off four more consecutive birdies.

On the 18th hole, she settled for par. Then, "I started to count quickly to myself to make sure I had shot 59," she wrote in *Golf Annika's Way*. Assured that her math was as good as her game, she jumped into the arms of her caddie. "I'm absolutely overwhelmed," she told the media moments later.

A Woman Among Men

The moment Annika announced that she would accept an invitation to compete against men at the PGA's Colonial Tournament in May 2003, a storm of controversy broke out around the golf world. "This is a man's tour," said Vijay Singh, a top player on the tour. Annika had plenty of supporters, too. Mostly, though, everyone was just curious to see how well she'd play.

Annika was understandably nervous when the tournament finally began, yet she regained her trademark cool once she pulled her driver out of the bag. "She began her round, on the par-4, 404-yard 10th hole, with a queasy stomach and wobbly knees and perspiring hands and a textbook par," reported Michael Bamberger in *Sports Illustrated*. She ended up with a one-over-par score of 71 for the day.

Overall, Annika did well again on the second day, but putted poorly. She finished at 74 and failed by three strokes to make the cut to play the remaining two days.

Still, thousands of fans cheered her every shot and treated her to the weekend's biggest applause when she got to the final hole.

Annika can't believe it after sinking the putt to win her third U.S. Open in an 18-hole playoff against Pat Hurst in 2006.

on the par-70 course, Annika failed to make the cut. Nonetheless, she gained a lot of positive recognition for women's golf and accomplished her personal goal. "I really tested myself," she remarked afterward. "That's why I'm here. I have a lot to be proud of."

Sparked by the positive experience, Annika added both the LPGA Championship and the Women's British Open that summer to her list of majors wins. She thus became only the sixth player in LPGA history to win all four majors and complete the so-called career Grand Slam. Later in 2003, she was named the *Associated Press* Female Athlete of the Year and became the first international women's player to be inducted into the World Golf Hall of Fame.

On July 3, 2006, after Annika won her third U.S. Open by prevailing in a dramatic 18-hole playoff against Pat Hurst, she had 10 career majors. Only Patty Berg has won more women's majors, with 15 (including three as an amateur) between 1937 and 1958.

"I've come a long way, and sometimes I have to pinch myself and say, 'Is this really true? Is this really happening?'" Annika told the media that joyful day. "I hope I have a lot more to give and a lot more victories out there — and hopefully some more majors to win. We'll see."

Most likely, we'll see Annika being interviewed after more victories, more majors, and more proof that she is the greatest female golfer ever.

Annika already is the best female golfer ever—and she's not done yet.

Annika's Career Statistics

Season	Events	CM	W	2	3	T-10	Best	Earnings	Rank	Avg
1992	1	1	0	0	0	0	T-64	–	–	77.0
1993	3	3	0	0	0	2	4	47,319	–	71.1
1994	18	14	0	1	0	3	T-2	127,451	39	71.9
1995	19	19	3	3	1	12	1	666,533	1	71.0
1996	20	20	3	2	1	14	1	808,311	3	70.5
1997	22	20	6	5	3	16	1	1,236,789	1	70.0
1998	21	21	4	4	2	17	1	1,092,748	1	*70.0
1999	22	21	2	4	3	12	1	863,816	4	70.4
2000	22	22	5	2	4	15	1	1,404,948	2	70.5
2001	26	26	8	6	1	20	1	2,105,868	1	69.4
2002	23	22	11	3	3	20	1	2,863,904	1	68.7
2003	17	17	6	4	1	15	1	2,029,506	1	69.0
2004	18	18	8	4	0	16	1	2,544,707	1	68.7
2005	20	20	10	2	0	15	1	2,588,240	1	69.3
2006#	16	13	3	3	0	13	1	1,668,216	3	69.9
Career	268	257	69	43	19	190	1	20,048,356	1	–

LEGEND: EVENTS: tournaments entered; CM: cuts made; W: tournament wins: 2: second-place finishes; 3: third-place finishes; T-10: number of top-10 finishes; BEST: best finish in any tournament during that season; EARNINGS: dollar total of prize money won; RANK: ranking on the LPGA tour money list; AVG: per-round scoring average for the season.

*Annika's official average was 69.99 before rounding up.
She was the first LPGA golfer to break the 70.0 mark in a season.

Through Oct. 1

GLOSSARY

auspicious   favorable or successful

drought   literally, a long time without rain; in sports, a long time between victories or championships

encore   a follow-up performance

flawless   perfect; without defects or errors

lingered   remained, or were slow to go away

par   in golf, the assigned score for each hole (or for a course) against which golfers measure their own scores

professional   a person who makes money performing a certain skill

renowned   well-known, or famous

rigorous   harsh, or hard to do

Scandinavian   coming from Scandanavia, a region in Northern Europe that primarily includes Norway, Sweden, and Denmark

scholarship   a gift of financial aid to attend college; when an athlete receives a scholarship, she (or he) agrees to play her (or his) particular sport for the school in return

scrutiny   close examination

BOOKS

Annika Sorenstam (Amazing Athletes)
By Jeff Savage
Minneapolis, Minnesota: First Avenue Editions, 2005.
Another look at the golf star in a book for young readers.

The Golf Book for Kids
By Jim Corbett and Chris Aoki
Seattle, Washington: Hara Publishing Group, 2000.
This book teaches youngsters about the history of the game and golf etiquette, as well as providing helpful golf tips.

KISS Guide to Playing Golf
By Steve Duno
New York, New York: DK Publishing, 2000.
A comprehensive how-to guide to playing golf from the creators of the "Keep It Simple Series."

Michelle Wie (World's Greatest Athletes)
By Jim Gigliotti
Chanhassen, Minnesota: The Child's World, 2006.
Some experts believe that this teen star may one day challenge Annika's supremacy among female golfers.

WEB SITES

Visit our home page for lots of links about Annika Sorenstam:
www.childsworld.com/links

Note to Parents, Teachers, and Librarians: We routinely check our Web links to make sure they're safe, active sites—so encourage your readers to check them out!

INDEX

ABOUT THE AUTHOR

Bob Woods is a freelance writer in Madison, Connecticut. Over the past 20 years, his work has appeared in many magazines, including *Sports Illustrated*. He has written books for young readers about Barry Bonds, Shaquille O'Neal, NASCAR history, and other sports topics.